domestic interior

PITT POETRY SERIES

Ed Ochester, Editor

domestic interior

Stephanie Brown

UNIVERSITY

OF

PITTSBURGH

PRESS

Published by the University of Pittsburgh Press, Pittsburgh, Pa., 15260
Copyright © 2008, Stephanie Brown
Manufactured in the United States of America
Printed on acid-free paper
10 9 8 7 6 5 4 3 2 1
ISBN 13: 978-0-8229-5997-7
ISBN 10: 0-8229-5997-6

To Nate

Double Thunder, God's Gift

Is there any part of life that is not sad, cheerless, dull, insipid, and wearisome unless you season it with pleasure, that is, with the spice of folly?

Erasmus, *The Praise of Folly*

Contents

Part III: Folie à Deux

Part IV: Not Too Serious

Part V: The Mother

neighbors

I Observe This Morphic Field

They were potato chip eaters.
Hearty laughers, the kind that make you go deaf and then you can't hear the
    entertainment.
I hate that kind of laughter, don't you? Or not, maybe, but I do.
They were TV watchers.
I mean they weren't embarrassed by all the hours.
I mean they thought back nostalgically to cute TV-kid actors.
I mean they said, "awwwww," when recalling this kid.
I mean they sang along to the theme song without ironic distance.
I mean, perhaps they were more innocent?
But, also, they got all worked up by the news shows.
I mean, they go, "Look at this crap!" and raise their blood pressure.
They felt what the *newsanchor* told them
So I thought of the proles in *1984* with their cheap stories, their sordid porno;
I thought of the rage induced, the violence toward the fake enemy that was
    their TV show;
I watched them rail against too-kind jail conditions, or later the unnecessary
    imprisonment of someone in maximum security;
They yelled at the TV and at the people in the room.
I watched them suddenly care very thoughtfully about the psychology of the
    movie star
Crying over it, crying.
But it clicks off.
And sleep is the sleep of beer and potato chips.
And sleep is the sleep not of distance or travel but of right there.
Sleep is the sleep they've been fed, like TV and potato chips,
Like food-porno: the beautiful high-fat burger glistening in its spin.
Once I saw them lick their lips in anticipation
Like my cat does when the cat food can is opened.
Honey, that made me unbearably sad, that lip-licking.
They watch a screen of tales that tell them
The world outside is full of beautiful people, hard times,
Frightening mountains and dangerous leopards,
That no one is to be trusted, that no river is clean.
But is the river clean, or isn't it?
What does the *newsanchor* say to it?
What does the *newsanchor* say to the river?

Domestic Interior

A loose cannon always marries a wet blanket,
And as they become one—one in the marriage, because in a marriage two
      become one—
Watch her: she will take on nervous, aggressive mannerisms,
and talk fast, and talk too much. Sulky dude, he sits there, slumped posture,
tree stump.
At first she loved the macho stuff,
And he loved her helpless breasts,
And her high laugh, and her dour, responsible lips.
She was an alarm clock, she made the bed.
She set him on the straight path, etcetera.
She folds the laundry as she lectures him about society, and how to write his
      resume.
His back folds, and he flips the channels, but he takes it all in.
At first she loved the macho stuff,
limp in his Popeye arms, his chest of steel;
his fist hurt and her head crashed when he threw her against the garage door.
And he softly fingered her black eye
When she cried it was wonderful
How close they felt. . . .
They sank into the soft forgiving mattress, year after year.
After a decade she talks like a motormouth,
She solves the car trouble,
She pays the bills,
She argues that she is right,
She keeps the blackmail safe in a safe in case she needs it.
He does not know the combination.
He is bad, that bad, bad boy.
But he never has to speak too clear, or be too much, or worry that she will not
put out.
Really, she still likes the macho stuff. He likes, he hates
her mouth.

Private School

To snub anyone effectively, one must have him within range.

F. Scott Fitzgerald, "A Freeze Out"

The mothers' wait
Is a time to visit, chat. Over there
She reigns, because she is delightful, trim, astute, kind, volunteers to feed
the poor, she comes in her
riding pants and riding boots, she arrives and a flock of wannabes flock around;
(She lives on the most exclusive street in town)

The snack today was brought
by Bernard,
who comes from another country, a rich one, full of zillionaires
And he has brought two plates, an artfully cut-up mélange of fruit, another plate
of finger sandwiches, all made at the Farmers Market Deli
Carried by the maid (or is she a nanny?) who is from another country too,
the Third World down the street. She brings the plate, signs her name in the space
under *Sally Fate, Marisa LeBray,*
which confirms she's dropped the kid off: *Maria.*

The volunteer today
wears Hermès.
She crashed the truck in Santa Fe!
What a weekend getaway!!
Oh my God! Oh no! offer
her loyal foes . . .
She is married to Fame and sometimes shows her belly button in too-tight clothes
Trophy for the famous prize—
Her husband, who never smiles, never.

Everyone wants to volunteer, even the Dads
Who are thoughtful, kind, respectful, polite, adorable, greedy, luxurious,
        glad-handing, varsity-level
wearing
the subtlest sportswear in vibration.
Their skin is creamy, dreamy.

Are you going to golf today?
Another mother asks the other Dad.
But he has already! That's great,

Etcetera, etcetera.
The kid (he says good-bye to his kid)
is *special special* Better than normal And this school is a special place
I don't know just filled with . . . do you know? Of course
each child is—innocent and soul-filled, sincere . . .

Everyone is *special*
And I think I am tired of that most of all: *special*
though probably the monthlong discussion of the marble wine-bottle holder
     was what did me in
Every day! Every day! Every day!
There is an auction where we must bid
in the $600s, the $700s for some kid's Mom's creation—
for the classroom contribution, I mean:
A basket of Gourmet, a blanket of cachet, a squirming basket of squid under a
     lid—

It's for a good cause, this spending, she says, the organizer who calls me calls
     me calls me *Don't forget!*
She has to talk to me, for the cause. Otherwise she might snub me
like her friends.
You gotta show your gottalottabux and if you don't have them you have to
Pretend.
I'll think about it, I said, the tickets, the auction. I'll think about it.
But I yanked my kid

And I hung my head in shame
And had to walk the other way: Adieu! At mid-semester,
Forbidden now to return, cast out—
I failed, I failed for us at private school . . . !
I said to myself, but not to my kid. I did not say,
A mother needs to be a powerful player, O child. Endure. Beware. No one
plays fair.

Bougainvillea

The simple things.
The simple life.
Can we buy one? Can we give it time?
The yard is sunny, on top of a hill. I'm amazed.
Don't worry. The sun makes heat.
The little flowers that need shade will not thrive here.
The deep pink gash, thrash, stainless beauty of the bougainvillea will survive.
Bloom and rebloom all year. Thorns along the side.
The petals fall into the kelly-green grass, into the clear clean glass-green water
        of the pool onto
the warm cement. Lie down there. And the wind
throws the petals all through the air.
They turn pink-to-brown under the rake.
Maybe you were alive someplace, in the East.
But this is not the East. Don't bring it around here.

Neighbors in Their Own Bunkers

The man in his bunker lets no one in
So the NO TRESPASSING sign is a given
On the high fence, with the curly barbed wire.
The gun rack, you guess, is not hidden,

Because you've never been inside to see it
and you will never, in a million years, go in.
Those family members who come out from their shrouds on occasion
look dazed by the sunlight.

Yet the smiling face of the Buddha
—(the man around the block, not a real prophet)
hides inside his sheepskins and his reputation
Even what he says is not what he says

Even what he does is not what he does.
The face is open and the house is open
And the collection displayed during the parties for four hundred
for the hospital and the children's orchestra. "Welcome."

The bunker, the bunker.
Lets no one in.
Lets no one see the wet oil stain.
Lets no one see the addendum.

How Could We Decorate a Haunted House?

These streets like a clogged cochlea
Low and deep and the houses follow up a narrow steep

Inside the haunted house the man sits and fills the whole room.
His sad and defeated drinking perfumes off his belly
His cigarettes and his ponytail
His rolls of fat, his bag of nachos
And the nervous woman in the kitchen
Greeting us, hello, to walk through this place at 6:45 in the morning
They want to sell—

Nearly hitting our heads—

The flocked wallpaper from a cocktail hour
A vista over the valley, though the traffic swirls up too loudly—
Like a nasty acrid smell
Wouldn't have been that way when it was built, when it was in fashion
And no one updated the appliances in all those years;
Door handles have fallen off, the wood paneling punched like a loud yell.

A guest with a prosthetic left leg swivels in his swivel chair to look at us
Highball glass in hand
Down the valley, lights across the land.
She was
The date of this available gentleman.
Now she is dead, the view of the town.
Nothing left: no furniture, no sweet satin nightgown.

Calm Down!

We were perfect, and we were perfect.
We were perfect people who had perfect parents.
And yet we were not perfect enough and we had to search
and we had to be self-conscious about our shapes and touch our hair a lot
and say, does this look all right? and spend the night
obsessing on our thighs, sucking in stomachs, our mouths: whatever
was wrong, standing in self-conscious touching of our poses
smiling and/or frowning too greedily, with too much hunger
and never letting go when we turned out the lights
and elsewhere of course our perfect lotioned minds
and our really bright rivers of discourse
were muddy and dirty and polluted
and we were always worried about being wrong
and we were always worried about the other guy
and how he was wrong and how we were wronged
and how we were fighting for justice
and how we were fighting for rights
and how we were arguing in court
and how we were arguing in kitchens, on car rides;
and how we were winning arguments
and how we were screaming
and how we were right, and how we were screaming,
and how we were right
and how we were screaming
and how we were right
and how we were screaming

Library

*There is not such a cradle of democracy upon the earth as the Free
Public Library.*

Andrew Carnegie

Potions and lotions, which all smell gross,
And regressions to the past, the past self
Pierced tongue, pink hair, potty mouth
Voodoo doodoo, Wiccan crap, fake religion borne out
Of the Englishman's loss of the oral trad.
Taken up by this Betty Page–tattooed elf
Doing spells via the Internet, which I can see
Over her shoulder——me——the neutral
Bringer-to-info in the building of the free
Housing and retrieval of information, and so I go
Like a psychopomp between
The conscious and the unconscious world, bringing her, and the guy
Who gambles away online
His Social Security checks each time and therefore sleeps on our patio
And help each one "log on" to "cyberspace"
Words invented by William Gibson, an American novelist, I believe;
And help them print their pages from the screen.
Here you go.
I stand beside, with no opinion, with no interpretation, and besides,
There is someone else now who needs a guide
To oil painting and here he needs
A book by an author that is translated from the Thai
Language and the fourth request today for *Romeo and Juliet* in pbk.
Our drunk walks to the front door carrying today's newspaper.
Excuse me, you can't take that out of here.
He is, he thinks, my pal. He pats me on the back: *I'm busted.*
I have no opinion.
I cannot interpret taxes. Here is the form.
I cannot give you advice for that, sir.
My mother has Alzheimer's. I need to know.
How can I find out about fetal alcohol syndrome?
The baby we adopted . . . I offer her a tissue
And we walk to the shelf.

This is just a house.
I will guide you between worlds—take this—here it is—
But now I must go.
Now there is someone else who needs
That stupid trashy book by a misguided author-freak that everyone's reading.
Yes, we have it.
I give it with no advice and no opinion.

Saying Good-bye to the World War II Generation

Francis was in a Japanese concentration camp for three years
And he was skin and bones upon his return to L.A.
And Bob stormed Iwo Jima and Okinawa and Tarawa
And Bill took the beach at Normandy on D-Day
While my dad and Walt had it easy in the Aleutians, though they were bored as
    heck
(It was not swell)
And every day, I think, growing up, my mom or dad said,
We thought that war would *never end!*
And there were all the friends of my mom who married guys
Because of how they looked in a uniform. It was unwise.

Francis, Bob, Bill, Walt, and Wives
look at the photos of my dad in his uniform.
This is in the vestibule before the funeral.
Their skin mottled and tan, their posture stooped, leaning on wives, or canes;
Except for Francis, a runner like my father, who stands pretty tall.
"You should have pictures of him running," he says, with a mouth-and-eyes
    smile.
My dad, the Miler. Record Breaker.
My dad smiles back, he is young. He is getting married.
He is a kid, twenty-one.
Under the photos we put out the flag we received from the post office
Because he is a deceased veteran.
But the secret is, he was really no flag-waver.
The army taught him he had to be his own boss.
He had never thought about it before much, but then he knew.
He had to be his own boss.
I think he told me that every day, too.

Old men, they look at the photos.
We stand and talk. We look. We look at one another.
I don't even know them much.
I was so much younger than my sisters and brothers.
I was the kid at the tail end, as late middle age crept in.

They are grandfathers, great-grand-men.
Not much can they hear, or see, the lights are too dim;
Their bodies carrying them past ninety soon enough.

The war they fought
Is not the war the grandchildren and the great-grandchildren and the great-
        great will fight.
It's time—
So they lay down their arms,
They lie down in their beds. Quietly,
Without complaint, they go as they went marching into battle.
Behind the hospital bedside curtain we close their eyes.

No Irish Need Apply

Dear Stephie,

Thank you for the birthday card.
Here is five dollars for you.

Love, Poppie

It made me weep—
the right word for it—
the jagged hand, the loose and careful eighty-eight-year-old's letters—
this note I found from when I was a grandchild.

❧

I didn't grow up with caricatures of ape-faced drunkards in ads;
nor was I accused of a Popish plot, wouldn't face life
as an old biddy or a wet-nurse
Because of the anonymous work of persons like my grandfather.
We did not think about shamrocks, letter bombs, or dark brew,
nor was anyone teary-eyed about the old country;
We lived far away from the three-decker neighborhoods
with Mary statues and drunken uncles.

❧

He was very, very old.
He was from another country.
He was ancient, and lived forever.
He always sent us money.
And of course there were Mary statues and drunken uncles, even in L.A.;
And bitter sisters who never, ever spoke again, not even
would their children, fifty years later.
(Money. And mother loved her better. And being high-and-mighty.)

Orphan, selling newsprint on the streets
Back East: the story.

The room is paneled in serene and deep wood—I don't know what kind—and
      the fire.
And he told us the story, but we never got the answers.
How old are you?
They sent the relatives boxes of oranges at Christmastime.
What happened to your father?
He was very, very old, even when I was a child.
How did your mother die?

Here's a dollar for you.

He ended his days in the hands of an angry offspring.

I never really felt anything.

And he kept his secrets.
He left the world with his secrets.
Here's a few dollars for you.
Buy yourself a new doll.

The other day I found a note and

—but I was little—will you forgive me, reader?

Not old enough yet to be grateful,
Not grateful yet that no one ever asked me to be grateful.
And that no one ever asked me to thank any lucky stars.
No Back East.
He was ancient, and he lived forever.
We had enough. We had a land of plenty.

Massachusetts

The land was ours before we were the land's.

Robert Frost, "The Gift Outright"

The City on the Hill held them:

Submit Hastings, Thankfull Sprague

Unite, Hepsibah, Renew, Ebenezer, Mercy, Patience, Experience, Devotion, Jane:

He was of the most profane family imaginable, the first hanged man in the colonies.

Hannah Haskins, dau of Samuel, died a Virgin, 1648.

He kept his horse saddled so that witchcraft trial victims could ride away in the night.

Here lies Israel Cox, a Revolutionary Soldier, aged 94 y. 11 mos.

That very large lady in the diaphanous white slip striding toward the west—
    do you know that painting?—

And yes, I think so, yes, I believe in it: free soil, freedom, progress, profits,
    streets paved in gold,
(the starving, the refuse, the refugees)

and radical, radical thoughts.

education

"Liking Something Is Not Enough"

Did their Catullus walk that way?

Yeats, "The Scholars"

All About Eve meant more to me than *Adam Bede*
But the teacher had taken his summer trip to see the authentic
"Mill on the Floss," & Hardy's Monument, & Austen's charmed cottage
And Cambridge full of Aprile
And a tour bus to Stratford-upon-Avon.

He had done his homework.
We watched his slides on the white wall of room 25.
And that teacher was bigger than I was
At age fifteen
And at age nineteen
And at cum laude day in Boston.

Who is your hero?
Write a five-paragraph essay and begin each with a topic sentence—
High school—
So I wrote, "David Bowie," and then I wrote, "or maybe George Carlin."
I failed to see what the assignment was about.
Well—my friend who got an "A"
Wrote about her mother—her divorce, her struggle
To pay the rent, her moment of truth at the Suicide Hotline.
I never got these things right: how to understand the secret assignment.

Then, you know, I moved on to Skeltonics and Romeo
While at a matinee I watched
The *Macbeth* that was Roman Polanski's
and I really, really loved those witches
but how to say it—to the Shakespearean scholar who is
so very, very unconcerned with that image?

You've made your point here. I don't think your "argument" is convincing,
It said in the margin, and also—well,
look at my title again.
Funny when you're young how you keep trying to convince yourself.

Because while you're getting formally educated you can't say,
Sorry, but I'd rather write about this campy Eve movie more than the campy George E.
And for a while you probably shouldn't even think it.
But eventually . . . eventually I suppose you should get used to the stares,
and you should say it, i.e.,
I loathe the ending of *The Mill on the Floss*—what grimness!
And there's nothing better than Eve's fall.

FOR TONY HOAGLAND

Diagnosis: Psychosis

The locked ward is not full of
Full-of-life movie stars playing
Wiser than you or I wisenheimers
à la Sean Connery or Jason Robards or
the entire *Cuckoo's Nest* ward,
Full of righteous indignation the world killing their spirits
In a conspiracy against the truly sane who are
These people who choose not to "conform"; who
"take recreational drugs"; who
"fight the power"; who
want to have more fun; who
must break under the thumb of bureaucratic thumbs—those
underpaid nurses and distracted docs
who need to see these sufferers suffer more—as if
they would care that much. I cross the threshold into

The locked ward: full of the sick, full of illness; the life force
Drugged and not very lively—even in the completely out-of-control
Shrieking person I happen to be visiting. She is
Full of words which don't make sense and I know by now
She will not teach me anything about my spirit that I have not learned
Inadvertently from her already, nothing that I do not know.
The two burly men who have been hired
For their biceps and triceps
Keep her from running out the door which has opened because I have entered.
The locked ward is where you go after you've tried to off yourself
Where you wake up instead of having died
—and I agree, she has nothing much
to live for—
and this is the sad thing. There is no one who cares much besides
compulsory compassion like the kind I bring along with a bag of toiletries.
(Though I cried with *pity* watching the way
her starved and skinny body ate chocolate ice cream
a week or so before the *suicidal gesture* that brought out the ambulance.)
Do you want

A visitor or not? the burly man asks her. She thinks
I have come to liberate her.
I always betray her.
The nurses at the nurses' station shake their heads in unison-disgust
At this difficult patient, my relation, Blanche Dubois.
The burly man checks the drugstore bag for glass and razor blades.
—*This is a nice hospital.*
—*It's not a nice hospital.*
—*You can rest here and get better.*
—*I'm not staying here. There's nothing wrong with me.*
—*I brought you shampoo and things you need until the hearing on Monday.*
—*You should have brought me clothes.*
When it's time to leave, one burly man escorts me to the threshold
And one holds onto the arms of my relation
Who finds herself in such an unbelievable situation
—*I have a bunch of appointments I need to go to!* she calls to me
And she will miss them. She is a victim—
Of relations like me, and of the System,
And eventually all victims find themselves like this: locked up, not free.

Time, Waste of

There is too much conversation in the world
And no one who is quiet.
Everyone with a telephone planted onto or inside an ear
(and a water bottle to suck on, like a teat)
In Sav-On, in Rite-Aid, in MaxOfficeCoSpaceBlight, I overhear.

Those huge grins and head-nods and tight-lipped negotiations, or, better yet:
Let me share this—just let me just say this—look—my understanding is—
You phony, phony piece of shit.

Of course I am guilty of these things that are my culture, too;

Talked myself at least red, if not blue,
In the face. And wrote too many epistolary masterpieces to
Whom.
Who? People whose faces, now, I can't recall, whose names I can't remember.

See, e.g., Hildegarde, Fatima, Blake, McLuhan

The ditto sheet recopied each year was your teacher's piece of wisdom.
And it passed into e-mail bromides, borne long ago from broadsides
And the tales of palpitatin' wives.
And all these lessons have a piece of practicality and a piece of magic:
"Stop acting deliberately and start acting tragic," or
"Stop acting tragic and start acting deliberately," they confide.
No, no, they don't go back to the Pleistocene.
This is about the mind. Is it about the spirit?
There is kitsch spirituality as well as kitsch thinking, Bozolein.

"If you want to look thinner, you need to carry a big purse," she told me, casually.
    "I was reading that."
And I told her, "The abused stays with the abuser because she doesn't know
    better. That's what I read."
And in another time: "You can tell a witch by her demeanor," they all said.
And there was an account of the hanging in the popular press, in the urban legend.
And here it is again. Here is that story again. Here is that received wisdom.
And many have received visions:
Visions of the afterlife, the future, the past:
Castles and mansions, spirits—
Their words hang on them like talons, starting to grasp.

Invective

TO MY BELOVED ENEMY

The point is: F. You.
That's all it—(everything)—ever meant, ever.
That's all it's for.
It's a bummer how significant you grew
And how I so need to revenge you.
All I do and will do is a way to get back at you, to this I am dedicated.

I'd like to watch you really stew in your own shit,
when I pull off a complex psychological mind-f-er.
(Yeah, you can do it, though it may take years.)[1]
E.g., the point of my successful career as a _____ is F. You.
And the point of my unlined face is: F. You.
And the point of my sobriety is F. You.
And the point of my boob-job is F. You.
And the point of my twelve-year-old car and my million $ house is: F. You.
And the point of the beautiful new paramour?
So the old will say, "How could you!"
And the point of my unfailingly sincere smile is: F. You.
Oh, indeed, without you, my life has no meaning.
Oh, indeed, I wish you
Envy and covetousness;
Let me be the teacher who teaches you about your pratfalls and weaknesses!
Because then you could "eat your heart out,"[2]
You could grimace and ache with regret, bile, and gas pains.
I'd rather that you cry—don't *disappear* or *go very far away,* my lovely dear—
Who, then, would incite the throb of your varicose veins?

Sorry, you're not my type. Honey, get some help.
Okay—you were right about that—
So you told me—so I did—get help—
Oh yeah, I understand now,
Come 'n' get it—I get it all now—

1. (But it's worth it.)
2. This language is probably not *fresh enough* for you. Here: here's a head of lettuce for you.

It's all about: F. You.
You taught me that screw.
When the meek get their due,
They get a chance for: F. You.
And you were right—I was a loser, all right, and you, a hammer-on-anvil
        armstrong.
But don't gloat too much while you stand away your life on your
Rose Parade Float.[3]
Don't forget to make eye contact with your legions
Your lovers who loved your cruel maneuvers;
And still love you with unmentionable unreason.
Before you stumble
and cookies crumble,
before you look into my eyes as I say,
"You'll never know how much you meant to me."[4]
With a cold, new kind of smile.

3. Yeah, like this is really some *obscure* reference. Don't make trouble!
4. I will really be saying, "F. You." And thanks.

Prescription Pills

Her heart has run out of steam.
Her vitriol has run out of scream.
Her engine has rusted and died on the tracks like the strong nineteenth-century body
        that did manual labor.
That day is over.

We pretended for a long time, before we disappeared
Underneath our protective hats and sunblock.
Her face has the sunburn from the life lived at the campground
With wolves near the dry cleaners.

She may not come within one hundred feet.
She may not enter my place of business.
She may not call me next time from the holding cell.

Snobs

I was supposed to worship you from afar
Like a star
Admire your new car
Your cigar
Your aplomb, brusqueness, memory- and money-enhancing skills,
Your life that lacks any need for prescription pills blah blah blah;

I was supposed to understand that your superior children
Were superior in every way to my own
Mine, being mine, would be . . .

Reprehensible.
It was understood that I
was supposed to fawn over their deeds on playing fields and in school musicals
As if I were not mothering my own kids, buying my own cars
As if I were not wholly alive but in that state of mind played by the hired
Who play the role of service worker 8–5
There to receive your retail returns and diatribes on quality of service
They who pretend to be grateful to be in your presence as if

should some of your greatness fall on them like a drop of rain from a tree
and quench a parched throat, salve a dark soul as your soul shone

bright as the sun: a person should be merely grateful to receive that drop of
    water, that beam of
light, mi'lord, and curtsy.
I don't know if you figured out that I was merely being polite.
I was not worshipping you.
I was boosting your ego, I thought.
A smart thing to do, on my part.
Doing you a favor. Playing that part. Because we were thrown together
And this is what I did—like all service workers do—in order to survive my lot.
As if I did not have my own secret thoughts:
Thoughts about the superior state of my soul, my mind, and my art.

Marble Obelisk

Broken rich kids find a niche—like make-work given to the near-to-retiring.
Like employment behind bars, making jeans or license plates.
Little things where they file and smile to the other office mate
—"New shoes?"—
On their broken legs and broken feet
In a little hideaway on a fashionable street, someone's tax break.
Someone's foundation, a drug abuser's way station.

The broken plate walks from the car to the buzzer.
She holds on to the rail all the way to the door of the building
Like a scared, unprepared, untaught ice skater.
The large, powerful horsepower of the world behind her flat candy ass.
Stunted mind that goes around the spool of
how unhappy
how unhappy

Whole, serene, and distant God
knows what people will do for His money
and it makes him laugh, it is so pathetic, so predictable a phone call.
He writes a check to the broken plate
She dusts and polishes and waxes and frets over this paper heirloom
He leaves a will to her.
Don't be charitable.

She will cash the check and drink her falsely gregarious wines
And keep her tight self groomed and in low-heeled sandals.

The jealous, murderous god
Laughs
behind her hesitant her nervous her little instances of sexual terror.

She never had a home
Never had arms to fit around her middle
Never had to change a vacuum cleaner bag on her own
Still, and yet, dear reader, a few are so proud of her,
Making it on her own!
All alone, all alone.

Education

1. First Semester of College

We read about the !Kung Bushmen
And discussed the !Kung Bushmen in the essay in the class the next day
And no one ever asked why that exclamation point was in front of the name
        !Kung
And my professor sometimes called out my name
"Green" instead of "Brown," but he called on me, so that was one thing.
We read about the poor who had no address, so this made it hard to get a job
Because they had no address to write on an application
And I told my dad about this
And he talked about it to me at length and with great interest, which surprised
        me.
We did not talk about the poor, generally.
He gave free medical care to some cloistered nuns.
Does *anyone* choose poverty? I wondered, provocatively.

2. At the Prestigious Urban University

Sanctum Sanctorum
You may only bring in a pencil
You must relinquish your possessions in the foyer
And sometimes the incunabula you request brought out
—The rare book librarian himself
(only two or three exist in the world)
(only two or three scholars of his renown)
will appear—Why do you want to see this?
You must wear cotton gloves. You must stand there
While he turns the pages for you.
Thank you. Thank you. And again, thank you.
And so it was relatively blasé to bring down
Octavos from the sixteenth century
And sometimes I walked behind
The door that no one walked through
Because this was my home now.

On the streets the people would shout
Because they were insane and living hand-to-mouth
And in need of medical treatment.
I saw them every day, gave away change
Some days; some days I was too grossed out.

3. Another Home, Now

Children learn to spell *eggzam* as *exam*
They spell the word *speshul*
They buy toys for a quarter and a dime and a penny
And they divide eggs from eggshells.
Outside
The poor, crazy specter of my insane and mentally ill sister wanders around
And who knows where she sleeps and where she goes?
There is even a check for one thousand dollars waiting for her
And another one for ten thousand.
My father died. I have the children now.
I will never teach them everything I know, everything I've learned, everything
I've found out.

folie à deux

Pension, Venezia

He sized up their marriage: that it had been made from a handshake
And therefore she shouldn't say poetic, juicy words about her husband
(As she was doing, while marmalading her roll)
Because it was a handshake. Because it was a body-mate
And not a "meeting of true minds."
He overheard as he sat alone—
He overheard the wife's erotic language every day,
as their stay included a breakfast at numbered tablecloths.
They sat beside each other, as their room doors sat beside each other.
He heard the couple talk! And how they did!
So endlessly, into the night, and then they'd fuck;
He thought the couple were sort of stupid
Though they pretended to be educated
Though that was questionable, as he tends to look askance at any Californian's
    education.
They talked like gum-chewers, like badasses.
He was a man who whiffed decorum and so on—
If he sat on a chaise it was a *shez* and so on—
And he noticed that the couple had affected the German habit of saying "and so on"
While talking to some English-speaking Germans at the table to their right.
"They sound like mannered, enthusiastic idiots," he marveled,
"And they're making inaccurate and lame-o interpretations of American
    presidential politics."
They were not quick-witted but wholly and fat-tissuey sincere and earnest
Like Americans are—
With their practical, cringe-inducing, sexual marriages.
While he was, well, he was—
While the couple was so *unpoetic* and *unjuicy*. They were so
—I mean, they were really, really *low.*

Not that he, my creepy, green-ugly character, would choose any of these words
to marinate his frisson-minded mind in:
juicy,
lame-o,
badasses

fat-tissuey sincere and earnest. The wife—a plea bargain in a dress—
Sees that he does not suspect his very-pronounced candy-assness,
Or that his raiment speaks of the Roger Moore-era-James-Bond-fop;
He thinks to quote the Gordian Knot of the Peloponnesian Wars is a delicious
   appetizer
on his way to dazzle, erection, execution,
When he cheats on his wife—
who, who, who—well, she is a perfume-gift type.
(He pegs the couple as the type who think *germane* is an intellectual's word,
and knows that they eat deep-fried.)
Her rolls split open and the butter laid on
Morning *Buon Giorno!* with coffee;
And then the wife of the couple
She says the Italian phrase, in Spanish, all wrong.

And so what do you think of the picture I've drawn?
I can't end it here, can I?
I have concluded nothing, given you nothing to chew on, nothing

To bite, to take away and love.
Who is "in love" and for what reason?
What is a marriage?
Maybe this is the couple's honeymoon?
Why do we travel to faraway places?
Why do I portray that all-alone man as an asshole?

Ten Years

If the exclusive formula helps me,
I will not crack like glass.
My husband does not believe in taking measures and steps.
(Because I still believe in them?)

A relic, self-help.

I grew up and I believed in my capsules.
Of course all these cures and fakes and quacks
Go back many more generations than the one that I remember. Yes, yes, I know.

Does my specialness make me unique?

I am a jewel-like, multifaceted multitasker.
(But he would never compliment me on that!)

When I was contemplating something accusatory I remember
An actual voice inside me said,
(But you know it isn't true)
But really the neighbors spied on me and listened to me through the baby
        monitor. Yes, yes, it's true.

My husband sits like the Pope, enthroned, lying in his bathtub
"the unconscious is . . ."

and he runs with it.

He was a very talkative, cheerful, enthusiastic, jovial briefcase-toting type,
when we met, this Pope.

He closes his eyes, and there he goes, not believing in enthusiasm, or being
        talkative.

He knows it was all about fear, nervousness, fear of nervousness, nervous
    feelings of fear.

His afraid-self married my false self.

O the wedding: soup to nuts!

Yes, yes: Now what?

No, no, no: I did not
*lightly trickle my fingers in the warm bathwater. "Honey," I didn't say. I didn't make that
line of dialogue which for instance leads the reader back to the beginning image of our
broken front porch, emblem of our marriage, and now we get out the hammer and nails
to fix it. You see, that is not happening. And the husband wants to build bridges and
houses within his own body; he sees this as fixing windows and he needs to repair his soul
and body but the wife wants maybe to wear a beautiful dress and be admired for her jewels
and the way she walks across the floor of a crowded cocktail party. She wants numerous
people to walk into her home and comment on the loveliness of everything. He is fixing
something else*

The Temper

There is the husband, the wife, and the temper.
There is the house and the driveway and the cracked, declining cement, and
    the temper.
The front door, the glass bowl, the temper.
A bill on the table. A key to your heart.

Furry cheese and a spilled-open box of rice.

No tape—*enny*where in this entire house—!

The doctor, the wife, the temper.

Can you help the temper?
You plead with the temper.
You disagree with the temper.
The rage-filled phone message and the silent sex and the temper.
The tiptoe-on-eggshells around the sleeping giant (*Shhh! The temper!*)
Wake while the temper sleeps. Sleep when the temper breathes.
Cajole the temper.

The dentist's reminder card.

Creeping bacteria, whistling teapot.
Scrubbing grout with a toothbrush.

The temper grieves in a dark little homestead,
Place of questionable diseases, real debt.

A drawn-shade, pajamas-all-day kind of place

Confused, confused regret.
"NO."
The temper always says that.

The Alcoholic and the Ball and Chain

He takes her on a date—a "date," a "surprise!"—
But nothing's planned.
It's just another requirement, like passing a written exam.

Another night with the wife.
He doesn't even know what to write
So there's no card. An unwrapped box—here—this's for you.

What she wanted.

Did she get what she wanted?
This is the way she looks at life—so he calls her a child
When they fight.
He's putting in his time with her—
Before the bottle of beer (her disapproval, her smirk)
And the bong hit (out of work).

Legal Separation

We live in a jail.
There is Plexiglas between
We talk into the telephone
We are not allowed to scream
Because if we do we are sent to Solitary.
Because, in the plea bargain, we agreed.

Heads bowed and walking to our balanced-diet, state-supplied dinners.

Talking over the metal trays
We parry and thrust and we are tough and nearly dead.
Numb and speechless
After we have talked out the agreement
Lawyers on one side, papers between

Heads bowed and walking to our cells.

Punishment feels like extreme boredom
The judge says, the judge says.
Wait. Just wait. Just *wait!*

Follow the rules or face the consequences.
The consequences will cost a lot of money, and time inside the courtroom, I
    assure you.
We could ask for help. I assure you.
We could become jailhouse lawyers. I assure you.
We could become recidivists, career criminals. Many trips to the cell.
We will make acquaintance with inmates from adjoining parallels.
Everyone has a story to tell.
Rehabilitation is rare—a gold nugget, a clear blue sky, someone waiting for
    your return from hell.

John Barleycorn

Here's a sad song for you—

What happened was the man *had* to— . . .
There was the wife who
Soaked it in through her skin—;
Every bit of his madness and sadness
belonging to the man who could not cry.
And then there is a crazy bastard boy,
The one starting the engine in the car inside the garage to die,
And the freaking rage and shouting,
the sobbing and hysterical tears,
Cuts on the skin with knives.
And institutions that take them in
and jails and rehab and inpatient and halfway.
This story never ends. Never dies. Keeps taking
hostages to the legend.
Don't ever think you're safe, it says to me, to you.
Don't ever believe
you'll be in any place nice
for any significant while.
Police, mug shot. Don't
smile.

That was a sad song for you who have gone now. Farewell. Good-bye.

After the End, Hope for the Beginning

Sometimes I had the feeling of someone choking me.
I would lose my breath to a phantom.
That was weird. Then
I was thrown back inside myself
the way a body is slammed by another into a wall.

I've seen that. And my bruised forearms.
I had to hide them with long sleeves for a few days.
Don't worry, it didn't happen in slow motion.
It's over quickly. It *smarts*. For a few minutes.
And then it's done. Can't be undone, like words
that can't be unsaid——. Never again,
he said.
The rest you carry in your dreams, and flesh them out
year after year, until they leave the body for good—the way,
eventually, a bruise heals without a scar.
And they do leave you, dreams, they do: that is what hope is, please God,
let that be a true thing.
Daisies, now, are what I dream about.

I look back and shudder.
Now I am a convert so I speak to the converted. I say,
"I'm being followed and racing to reach the leaving train.

I'm being followed and racing to the entrance of my house.
Quickly, Gretel, quickly, open up and climb to the tower
and lock the door. Rapunzel's lover

fell on flowers and the thorns blinded him. He wandered
the desert
but love gave him sight, to see, again."

Peace

Peace comes after the war.
Not before—we didn't know there was peace.
We weren't sure war was coming, but it felt funny.
There was an urgency to have the good time had by all.
Peace. The wreckage. The new house from the broken beams.
The work.
It's never forgotten, as the hammers go on from 7 to 7
And the burned toys picked out from the ashes.
The rest of the mess taken to the trash with gloves on.
And the good time had by all—
There in the mess—
Peace is not a time of rest, no.
I leave you peace, my peace I give you,
They say each week
When I go to meditate on the war, the waste, the thing.
And we are told to take the peace out into the world with us.
The mess I cleaned up, the hammers from 7 to 7, but it's over.
Go on.

The hard times are over: let the bon temps roulez.
I wish it could be that way.
But no matter: Mardi Gras came and went and now it is Lent.
I went and buried the dead.
I ministered to the sick: he lay detoxing each afternoon till six.
I had lived on Easy Street, honey, don't ever forget it.
It will never be the same for me again, don't doubt it.

Now it is time to pull down the shades and work deep into the night.
Go on.
Peace be with you. Don't fight.

not too serious

Self-Portrait at the End of the First Half of My Life

What can you do? You get these Mae West hips
and Jayne Mansfield breasts to succor with
And everyone thinks you're gonna be motherly:

Friends, boyfriends, cats, addicts, dolls.

But I had no "issues";
I knew I'd issue kids.
This was something that just is.

[The condescension one can give to the barren and all of that nasty shit
The "sainted mother" (a soul-killer) that comes with my genetic history.
None of that!—and that, I guess, is motherly.]

But I wanted to be more like the color of steel,
like the kind made at my grandfather's company,
Hard, smooth, and cool like the flat and hipless;
And so it is that I wanted to be a "some like it cold" type—
As I once read that Ring Lardner said or wrote
In Marshall McLuhan's *Mechanical Bride* of long ago.

[And somehow the world has forgotten "momism" of several generations back;
See, e.g., the generation of Ring Lardner;
And they've resurfaced—
Career moms, heart attacks.]

I wish I'd known that I could have been instead like a superheroine
Big boobs and thighs and boots all busted up and fighting crime
Holding aloft a sword and looking for a fight,
But curvy and stacked, all right.
I wish I'd known—
I could have seen my cartoon-like-inflations like that
And I would have stood up straighter
And I wish I had known that I could have been seen like a woman painted by
     Roy Lichtenstein
Fake and wonderful and titty and comic-strip lips.

Ah, regrets!

49

Not Too Serious

The dead poet started speaking to me,
Giving me funny lines to use in my writing.
The voice would say, no! no! when I tried to get too serious.
He liked me to stay light.

I then had the opportunity to meet Mr. Griffin
who had written a significant monograph on the dead poet's lines.
I·made my symbolic ablutions,
Reviewed my notes for the test,
and met Mr. Griffin at the dead poet's request.

But the dead poet had also spoken to Mr. Griffin
and told him this: "She is an opportunist."
I wondered why he had bothered to bring us together at all, if he would say that!
"I suppose he is a playful spirit and playful is not always kind or sincere, no?"
I said to Mr. Griffin, Mr. Snidely Whiplash.

But soon enough the spirit got annoyed with me
because I spent a long year hand-wringing, wet-blanketing, crying, and acting
      hysterical.

A year passes.

"Lighten up, you loser!" he said, whenever I tried to resume our conversation.
When I asked him to come back, he did not reply.
I wanted more funny lines!

Three years pass.

One night, walking among the lights of Christmas cheer,
I saw a man in a gorilla suit playing a valve trombone, all alone, in front of a
      multiplex.
It was a wet, mildewy, ocean night.
He wasn't asking for money, just playing.

"Dead poet, look at that!" I called,
hoping to impress him with the world I noticed—
but he was already gossiping about me to Mr. Griffin

And another year turned around.

The Staff Lounge

Case History A: Participant

You didn't need a graphologist's mail-order degree to see that her handwriting
    revealed her craziness.
You only needed a half hour of her discussion of romance to feel the doomed
    ending coming soon
The debt he left her with,
The accident, how he fled into the moon.
The loops where there shouldn't be loops, the tight spots that should open
    smooth, the big dots for the I
she learned in junior high.
You didn't need a nineteenth-century degree in medicine to diagnose her
    hysteria
Behind the mask of her set smile of 1950s American teenage life
With its belief in virginity and hysteria
I didn't believe in hysteria or craziness, see; I was the child of another era
Where these were *normal responses to a world gone crazy*
(Of course we lost our virginity in seconds!)
But after a while I began to disagree,
Siding thereafter with the Patriarchy
E.g., I could imagine wanting to shut her up, to beat her, I could imagine
Why she could become anyone's willing victim
And why I would scream
And why I would divorce her: *the normal response to a woman gone crazy*
And why she could thereafter only find con men to use her
And why she was crazy and loony-tunes and the whole bit,
You didn't need to drill holes in her head to let the medieval
demons escape; there were several that just came right out of her mouth
as she shape-shifted her posture
rigid
and spun around and around and around
A problem! A problem! A problem! And I, I am sure she nearly died
when she prayed for my hard,
bored, insensitive
heart. Because she told me: *I prayed for you. I cried.*

Case History B: Observer

She was from the generation where *if you can't say something nice, don't say anything at all.*
So her coworkers always knew when she didn't like something, because she wouldn't comment.
And he was from the generation where you tell a pretty girl, *Let's see a smile!*
So you can imagine the offenses . . . legal and otherwise.
And the youngster was from the generation where *you confront your perpetrator head on!*
So you can imagine the pain she caused for the *if you can't say something nice* lady with her
Number One Grandma! coffee mug steaming in front of her teary eyes the day she was told off . . .
(Bewildered, for she's never even had the *desire* to hurt anyone!)
And the youngster's friend, with the sprouts-and-cream-cheese-on-squaw-bread-sandwich-every-day
(She'd lived in an ashram, she'd acted in L.A.)—
She looked up from her biography of Beryl Markham,
She said, *Whatever turns you on. Live and let live.*

C. Follow-up: Coaching and Counseling

Define the conflict in the staff lounge culture.
How do we resolve it?

The Divorce of Mr. and Mrs. Moore

She was a serious bore
And he couldn't take it anymore
He walked out the door
He settled the score

He talks folklore to a whore who does her chore.

On the foggy seagully sandy shore
She implores the Gods. She tries to ignore
Advice, gossip, lies, and lore.
Her friends have told her about the whore and Mr. Moore
And there are surely more lies in store—
She wells up: "This can't go on anymore."

Very Tired, he sleeps on the floor,
The TV chiaroscuroing his canker sore-d
mouth. Open, snore.
Nightmare: 1-bedroom. Deadbeat-Dad-Poor.
He's laid out like a lamb before

The ritual: his heart to be torn open—blood and gore
And guts and buttery popcorn from the store.

That day that begins the divorce, the last day of *l'amour*.

Camp

When people ask—a get-to-know-the-new-kid work-conversation—"when's
    your birthday?"

Sometimes I say, "March 23rd,"

And sometimes I say, "March 23rd, the same day as Joan Crawford's."

Because that person may get the joke; we can
Dually recall:
Faye Dunaway sitting at one end of a table
Pepsi businessmen leaning elbows on the table
Listening in fear and irritation
And her eyebrows and her perfect Joan lips
Because she says, "Don't fuck with me, fellas!"
It's a laugh-out-loud moment when she says that—
And sometimes I muse aloud to the person who asked me for my birth date:

If we share the same birthday, do I share the same qualities with Joan?

If that person got all this. Maybe like
Joan, I'm the kind who winks when she says shit.

So I suppose when I say,

"March 23rd, the same day as Joan Crawford's,"

I am testing that person to see if that person can detect
This, too: *Don't fuck with me, fellas.* It's true.

The Satanists Next Door

What is that? Is that a kid? Is that Tom?

No, it's her.

Eew, I think that's a whip.
No, it's a hand coming down hard.
No, listen, there's like a wind-sound to it.

I need to go to the bathroom.

That one was fake.

Are you still awake?

She probably has to do that to get him to finish.
Listen: he sounds like an angel.
No one has ten orgasms in twenty minutes.
I can't tell.
Oh yeah, a lot of those were fake.
They're up all night doing meth and they have to have sex all the time.

Should we do it now?
Did that make you horny?
No, but we *are* awake. In fact, it's creepy to hear people.
She's a moaner.

It's getting light out.
Close the windows.
The seals are barking. I like that sound.
Can you hear the parrots?
Oh, yeah.
They live across the street in the canyon.
I think I smell that chemical smell.

Close the windows.
Do you think they ever put spells on us?
Whatever you think is happening, it's not happening.
It's all a lie.
Um hmm.

It sort of scares me.
Freedom of religion.
Yeah, you're right.
And we have the Jehovah's Witnesses on the other side. It balances things.
I'm going to put a holy card of St. Michael on the fence between us.
God will protect us.

Turn on your side.

Supervision

They think about me all day.
No, really, it's true.
When I walk in the room, they *oops,*
Because they were just talking about me—seriously—
I look across the room and the two of them are looking at me and talking—
About me—they're laughing now!
I wander in the lunchroom
They turn their backs, they're taken aback because I've walked in
On another conversation about me.
I swear to you, this is true—
All day long they think about me—
When I speak, one particular person lets out a gigantic sigh
My requests are met with rolling eyes—
All day long they do their voodoo
They obsess on me all day long. I'm not kidding!
Really, it's true. I have to go in and ask for something.
I have to show no fear.
They have to do what I say.
Some in there smile very hard and flatter me each day.
They think about me all day, too.
Each obsesses in her way.

Husbandry

Every time he does it: *"GET OUUUUT!"* like the ghosts in *The Amityville Horror*,
I laugh. I still laugh at it.
Hanging out in the kitchen, feeding the kids fried chicken.

Our kid was explaining St. Patrick's Day to us.
He heard in school about a dance the Irish did.
"Oh see, like this—it's called a jig—watch."
Dad's mesomorphic, 200 lb. body is now jumping. Arms go up

And down, feet skip high, land down
Careful-like. Leprechaun. Breathless: "You want to try it?"
He and the kid jig. "You got it!"

And he will demonstrate
A headstand too—"here, watch this!"—when needed.

Dolphins

Neon dolphin jumps in threes—his snout, his middle, his tail.
Starfish with a smile on his face: blinks on and off.
Baskets. Beach towels. Bikes.
In the window of the store that sits on the highway.
And here is the church and here is the steeple set atop the steep gray shale.

And the shale has steps down a cliff.
The steps covered by a bower of flowering trees that grow together and make a
     tunnel
Follow me

~~Now you can see the sea~~
Now you can see the expanse
Now you can hear the waves break on Seal Rock and then creep over sand.
The seals sleep a lot. The seals bark. ~~The seals sleep. Seals on a rock.~~

The lifeguard in his red trunks looks through binoculars
Stands on the number 5 tower
Looks to the water.
          This is my town, my own—
(Striped umbrellas, kids dig holes and run, the jogger, the dog walker on the
     railroad path,
The railway between San Diego and Santa Barbara. The train whistle.)

          This is my home—
The real dolphins, look at them! There they are today!
Some people even stand up, and point, and say
Look. Dolphins. Look!

And the artist in a straw hat stands at his easel
By the railroad tracks
Pacifically painting all day.

Roommates: Noblesse Oblige, *Sprezzatura,* and Gin Lane

How I recall that all her friends were "enormously gifted" and "exceedingly
　　bright."
I was a dim bulb.
Perhaps I knew a "gifted thief."
This was implied
As she was of the Social Register of NY
And I was from Cal-i-for-Nigh-ay, and we were, unfortunately, Back East.
I'm serious!
I'm serious as a heart attack, my train-riding-addict-hobo boyfriend used to
　　say, too often.
Whoops, oops, I proved her case.
Her aforementioned friends were working on committees for political reform
　　and election to public office
And I was of a lower class, yes, indeed—*arriviste*: lower, really, than the
　　working class, with all our
Pretentious collecting,
Belief in merit, college degrees, and not birth,
Belief in profits, not savings,
Bestowed on each succeeding generation like the sky and the earth.

Unlike her, though,
I liked my boyfriends really, really low,
I liked the criminal class,
I liked the suffering and the drinking,
I liked the violence, the big shrieking,
And the jail time, and the thinking.

(Show off! Show off! Show off!)

The Family Jewels

Cock stiffie woody plug
Skin-flute boner wiener hot dog
Hard-on fatty rod
Get it on
Hit a home run
Get next to you (Whispered: I fell for that one)
Go all the way
Wet your whistle
Lizard
Love-gun
O Play the field, Mr. Thomas, John;
And Willy, Dick, and Mr. Schlong,

Give the dog a bone
Dog-style, backdoor knock—
Or missionary: let her
Lie back and think of England.
Knock boots, boys
(i.e., nuts stones cojones nards);
One-eyed-wonder-worm meet

the little fellow in the canoe
& make him stand up
& Eat at the Y:
bearded clam
fish taco
sweet spot
cherry pie!

the mother

Hope for the Hopeless

I.

These were the diagnoses, in no particular order,
Not in chronological order—
In roughly alphabetical order, in order to recreate that six-month stretch of time:
- Alcoholism
- Alzheimer's Disease
- Major Depressive Disorder
- Type 2 Diabetes
- Drug-induced Psychosis
- Paranoid Schizophrenia
And the prognoses: divorce; incarceration or committal; shots three times a
    day; certain death.

And the outlook: hopeless.

And the way it felt: like I was going crazy myself.

The sun shines on the wicked as well as the good.
Let the day's business be enough for the day.
I didn't write those lines. Maybe nothing I ever wrote was really mine.
There is nothing new under the sun.

There is a grief so deep—well, it was my turn to feel it, being a human being—
I mean, where I fell off my chair one time—can you believe it—?
I mean, I cried myself dizzy, I cried vertiginously
I prayed with every cell in my body to get through one night one time;
I mean, despair.

Tears come at night but joy comes in the morning.
I didn't write that line.
I didn't write those diagnoses on the medical charts
Though those of us, around the patients, had spoken those names, anecdotally,
    many times.

II.

Each week for years I had heard the voices sing
—those naked lightbulb, those homely Sunday voices—
"Hope for the ho——ope——less!"

I always sang along. I sang that happy song.
Sunlight drifts in just right through stained glass, and I noticed that.

But during those six months I could not sing, could not
Open my mouth.
Though I still sat among them, and closed my eyes.
Sometimes I cried.
I let myself be carried on the voices of the others in the room.
I let myself be ferried across
As I could not lift myself, myself.
(Some can heal, you know, and some cannot.)

It was all I had—*and I mean*—it was all I had:
That verse that I did not write,
that song.

Indoors

I knew anger was a seven deadly sin because I knew her.
Rage filled the house, lifted the curtains, fell asleep in the food,
Woke up in the squealing tires of the car
While I lived in my soundproof booth.

*

When the helping starts, the forgive, *please* forgive—
You are doomed. Everything you said
can and will be used against you, next session, next sin
If you dare to agree that she behaved badly.
Don't agree! Let her believe she is the sweet fool that she is.
Every honest word, every real thought you had
must not be had.
There is no help, don't fool yourself,

*

run away, join the circus, hop a freight train, sign on for a sea voyage, hitchhike
     with a stranger

down the highway: there's a reason for stories like this one, and she is the reason.

The Devouring Father

He has a low, wicked laugh
His belly is a melon cut in half
He is fat because he has eaten all the children.
Beware, young child, who wants to be a pilgrim—
Dad is walking after you; Dad's a-comin';
Dad's shoes fall heavy on the linoleum,
Heavy in the carport,
Heavy in the syrup-odored pancake shop.
Smack you across the chops.
Smack you. You little asswipe dumbfuck.
Smack you. Belt. Make you without memory and dumb.

Mom lets Dad eat the children
Because she doesn't know what to do with 'em
Because she hates 'em but doesn't want to murder them herself
(That would have made her a monster, instead of a long-sufferer!)
She lives in a shoe; she doesn't know what to do. Get rid of some!

All along the freeways, the mountains and byways, the streams and rivers on
        God's green earth—
Dad's a giant walking after you
His weight, his shoes, his growl fall heavy on the trail—
His six-foot-long strides soon get him where he needs to go:
He smells you, he follows you, he puts a hand on each side of your neck—;

But if you don't die, if you survive
To tell the tale, tell it:
"The monster was really there. He was supposed to care
About me, but I fled and made my kingdom elsewhere."

Keeping

Straightening the bed. Straightening the drapes.
Righting the spilled cup of milk. Scrubbing the spot that it left.
Hating the stain from the sticky juice, and the shoe left its dirt there too
So it's dark in the light carpet and it can be seen more clearly at night under
      ceiling lights.

Polish the table, vacuum the crumbs.
A peace inside, a war won.
Lovely sound of water spreading through the dishwasher.
Put the toys in the toy box. Put the toys out on the floor.
Put on one shoe and then the other.
Let the children out.
Placing the wet laundry in the dryer.
Folding the laundry.
The delays of wet laundry.
Days of wet laundry.
Folding clothes for a quiet hour.

Sweeping routinely; the crisis of something shattering.
(shit)
Mopping: the floor is now breathtaking.

Sitting still, still sitting.
Watching the children alive jumping in their limbs outside
In the mown grass, inside the locked gates, safe here
To scream, to dig deep, to furrow the toys of commerce
(trucks, trains, bulldozers, cranes)
through wet mud in Spring

Climb loud screams and laughter
And a cry so loud it hurts my ears run to me through the sliding glass
I hold one until he's done with his screaming
I hold his body firmly against my own

I hold one and then the other who didn't fall but needs the embraces to be evenly
distributed between;
Now he's over it and wants to get down
Now the other is over it and wants to get down
The straightening of what they leave behind them as they run.

Coloring Book

This generation draws the lines.
This generation draws inside the lines.
This generation draws outside the lines.
This generation gets rid of the lines.
This generation cries "wee wee wee" all the way home.

Then the kids of the "wee wee wee" generation draw the lines.
And then their kids draw inside the lines.
And then the next generation draws outside the lines.
Then the next generation gets rid of the lines.
And the next generation cries "wee wee wee" all the way home.

St. Dymphna

Patron saint of those who suffer from nervous disorders

1.

Her lily, her lunatics
They founded a loony bin in Gheel, near her shrine
Escaping with her confessor, the wife, and the court jester
Away from the evil Father, King, Wanter.
Dymphna died,
But the power of her grave cured the sick of mind
An adventure story for the unkind truth
(Daddy tried to do her)
Before she ran away and died
(Daddy wanted to screw her)
An unsullied mystic, a fill of faith
(Daddy tried to kill her)
Dymphna is our patron saint.

2.

I saw them on a friend's kitchen counter.
I hide my SSRIs under my stockings and underwear.
She confided to me about her SSRIs, so I told her about mine.
I had hoped someone would be surprised, but no one really was.

"You? You?" But no one said that.

Can I stay on SSRIs forever?
Even though I know the cautionary novel about *soma,*
I said to the doctor, in the examining room:

I'm not kidding, it has been like a miracle.

So later, having found myself having said that word,
Miracle,
Out loud, I closed my eyes and said,
St. Dymphna, thank you.

Black and White

Nostalgia for Automats
Nostalgia for feelings we never had
The feelings of *Kitty Foyle*.
Nostalgia for black-and-white swing tunes
And spaghetti dinners in Greenwich Village
Chianti-bottle candles
The evenings of Kitty Foyle, descendant of *Back Street*
Plucky survivor, Kitty Foyle, attagirl;

Stand up and do not weep.
Brave, like Kitty Foyle.

Nostalgia for hats
And hatpins we never had
The hats and hatpins of Kitty Foyle.
Nostalgia for happenstance
Happenstance we never had
In front of our color TV set.
When I pretend, I pretend I'm proud, and brave, and Kitty Foyle.

"The Abyss Stares Back at You"

What doesn't kill me makes me stronger
was not a good time in my life.
I wasn't a young man in war I was just
a drinker with a confused life
with this as my motto;
Crows on the blacktop the day I drove to buy some painkillers—
That was my sunrise, my dream, my symbol.

Even the friendly checkout lady was a scary ex-con
The neighbor was a Peeping Tom
A guy in line at the store whispered "bitch"
as I went through the 8-items-or-less-line buying champagne and the
      aforementioned painkillers;
And through the change to a new motto
All the tears I had to let leave my body into some endless water cycle—
Clouds, rain, ocean, clouds, rain, ocean, river, stream, waterfall, lake
O deliver me, Lord, to a new day—

I cried so much, to reach a life which wasn't strength.

The World Will Ask for Your Greed, Envy, and Sloth

So write a hagiography of the day
And encomiums for the week
And thank the food that you eat
And remember fondly the bed where you sleep
And bless the fresh clean water in your spirit
And the dirty filthy dirt in your pockets
And the sunburn you took for going to the trouble of it
And the paper cut that gave you pause:
You are alive, abundant, filled
With seeds and blood, able to tame and thumb
A cat's soft life under your fingers—to be so kind, to be so loved—
There is a reason to write,
There is no reason not to write

A hagiography of that woman who went to serve street alcoholics in New York
      during the Great Depression
And who are you?
What have you done?

Good-bye

The house lets me take care of it
The way the boy never will
Doesn't know I need to take care of him
The boy pushes me away if I hug him
The chair lets me polish, wax, stands up straight
(unlike trying to teach the kid good posture!)
The pillow plumped fattened flattened
Hugged to put the case back on
Unlike the boy who will not let me hug him

"I know, I know, whatever," he says to my admonition: "Be good!"
Running from the car to summer camp
The boy who will not let me hug him
Does not stand up straight
(His hair stands up straight!)

Swim trunks long over knees the fashion
And strong tan back—"Okay!"—"Good-bye!"
I say.
"Good-bye, Mom,"
the voice a kid's so sweet like a solitary bird at 5 a.m.—

unaware, unafraid, and I
go back to the house that lets me take care of it,

unlike the boy who will not let me hug him.

Souls in Purgatory

Commuting.
Caution.
Rictus.

Tale of betrayal.
Nothing for her to do but listen to herself begin to tell the tale again.
Desk.
The warehouse superstores.

Headaches.
Fake laughter.
Not delivered.
Jaw aches.
Sitting.

Not even a clock to stare at.
Forgotten.

But there they are, and the day is the same day. And they are waiting.
And there you are with the clipboard, hesitating.

Whose turn is it now, for pleading, for you to listen?

Why won't you pray for them?

The Mother Becomes the Mother of Herself as Well

2.

My heart broke like a stone, thrown.
Or maybe this will help you to understand:
The ache was an insurmountable mountain climb.
So many steps, out of breath
Just have to give up, drop down to your death.

Little boy
Lower lip turning down Head lowered Eyes like starvation

Great granite mother am I.

My heart broke
Little boy
Christ, remove the log from my eye.
My heart broke, like a stone, thrown.

1.

On the way there I spent a long time
crying inside me, saying, "Mommy!"

Embarrassed, a real weirdo for doing that;
but I kept doing that
and I kept crying
All of it strange and I stood back and watched myself

As I was then watching myself do all things
in a monotonous, slow motion, cotton-candy,
get-nowhere way:
Put on the jacket,
and make the snack,
and smile the smile,
and give them a bath.

I called out for my mommy.

I was a baby, yes, and I am whining, now, yes, it's true.
But it's true, too.

And that's how a mother grows up.
And that's how a mother becomes strong, like a stone.
And like a stone, thrown.

Notes

In "Massachusetts": "The City on a Hill" refers to John Winthrop's admonition to colonists in New England: "For we must Consider that we shall be as a City upon a hill. The eyes of all people are upon us." The phrase was taken up by political speech-writers in the 1980s, unfortunately. "That painting" refers to John Gast's allegorical painting *American Progress* of 1872. Dedicated to my friend Jessica Hallowell Linley.

"The World Will Ask for Your Greed, Envy, and Sloth": "that woman" refers to Dorothy Day, 1897–1980. The poem was inspired by a book review of a biography (not about Dorothy Day) written many years ago by Joyce Carol Oates, who, as I re-call, coined the term *pathography* to describe a nasty trend in biographical writing to emphasize the worst parts of a person's character.

"Coloring Book" is for Judith Vogelsang.

Much dedication to Drbl.

Acknowledgments

Grateful acknowledgment is made to the editors of these publications, in which the following poems first appeared:

American Poetry Review ("The Abyss Stares Back at You," "After the End, Hope for the Beginning," "The Alcoholic and the Ball and Chain," "Black and White," "Bougainvillea," "Camp," "The Devouring Father," "Domestic Interior," "Education," "Hope for the Hopeless," "I Observe This Morphic Field," "Indoors," "Invective," "John Barleycorn," "Library," "'Liking Something Is Not Enough,'" "The Mother Becomes the Mother of Herself as Well," "Peace," "Pension, Venezia," "Prescription Pills," "Private School," "The Satanists Next Door," "See, e.g., Hildegarde, Fatima, Blake, McLuhan," "Self-Portrait at the End of the First Half of My Life," "Snobs," "The Staff Lounge," "The World Will Ask for Your Greed, Envy, and Sloth"); Kestrel: A Journal of Literature and Art ("Not Too Serious," "Ten Years"); Pool ("Calm Down!," "Roommates: Noblesse Oblige, Sprezzatura, and Gin Lane"); Slope ("Invective," reprinted in Slope 17); LIT ("The Family Jewels").

"Roommates: Noblesse Oblige, Sprezzatura, and Gin Lane" appeared in The Best American Poetry 2005.